Since the war [with Iraq] began, many people have told me that they long to pray about it but don't know how. Here is a book that guides us through wartime prayer in all its contradictory aspects. Jim Melchiorre—father, son, veteran, citizen, and man of faith—speaks honestly, with a moral energy and humility I treasure.

—BARBARA CRAFTON
Episcopal priest and author
Founder of the Geranium Farm, which publishes
the *Almost-Daily eMos*

Jim Melchiorre breathes life into an ancient spiritual practice that is desperately needed during this time of intense conflict on planet earth. In sensitive yet challenging ways, his book helps us reflect spiritually on an issue that weighs heavily on all people of faith. And it offers provocative questions we should wrestle with prayerfully so that we can act as ambassadors of God's love in this war-torn world.

—PETER WALLACE, author of *Living Loved*
Host of the *Day1* ecumenical radio program

This is a brave book. Brave in the raw and searching honesty that Jim Melchiorre brings to his subject. Brave in insisting that even a war far away is our war. Brave in bringing the personal face of battle right up to the door of our conscience and faith.

The novena is a beautiful way into this difficult material, perfect for groups, with probing questions that take readers to the ground zero of their faith and leave them there, deep in the heart of prayer.

—REV. SUSAN HULL WALKER
Charleston, South Carolina

Jim Melchiorre's work is prophetic and compassionate, thought-provoking and caring. He mixes pastoral concern with prophetic energy to create a powerful narrative for such a time as this! We need more people of Jim's caliber who walk the line of prophet and priest and stir the soul and challenge the mind. I highly recommend this book.

—REV. OTIS MOSS III
Pastor, Trinity United Church of Christ
Chicago, Illinois

Novena can most easily be defined as public or private prayers of devotion and intercession. As Jim Melchiorre explains in one of his prayers: "Picture a world where war is not an option. Think of all the human problems and disputes that would still exist but would need to be resolved in another way. Pray to God that you might play a part in that new world." That would be living the life of prayerful novena.

—REV. NICK ELLIOTT, Director
United Methodist Volunteers in Mission
Southeast Jurisdiction

Frances Helen Foley Guest

Novena in Time of

WAR

*Soul-Searching Prayers
and Meditations*

Jim Melchiorre

UPPER
ROOM BOOKS®
NASHVILLE

Cover design: The DesignWorks Group, Sisters, Oregon
Cover image: iStockphoto
Interior illustrations: Jim Osborn
Interior design: Gore Studio, Inc. / www.GoreStudio.com
First printing: 2007

Library of Congress Cataloging-in-Publication Data
Melchiorre, Jim.
Novena in time of war : soul-searching prayers and meditations / Jim Melchiorre.
    p. cm.
Includes bibliographical references (p. 85).
ISBN 978-0-8358-9940-6
1. Novenas. 2. Catholic Church—Prayers and devotions. 3. War—Religious aspects—
Catholic Church. I. Title.
BX2170.N7M45 2007
261.8'73—dc22   2007029993

Printed in the United States of America

for

PAUL JOSEPH MELCHIORRE

1920–2002

Contents

Acknowledgments

Writing a book is largely a solitary endeavor. Publishing one requires a team, and I feel honored and humbled by the contributions of my teammates.

Denise Duke answered questions about copyright and permissions with a skill surpassed only by her speed; an e-mail of inquiry to her at 10:00 a.m. would inevitably receive a reply and resolution by noon.

From Manchester, England, Kathleen LaCamera, my expatriate colleague in journalism, and from Nashville, Peter van Eys, our family's onetime pastor, both generously gave their time to read the manuscript and make valuable suggestions.

Indispensable recommendations for the books and papers listed in "Suggested Reading" came from our pastor in New York City, K Karpen; from Bud Heckman of Hartford Seminary; from Bud's longtime friend and mentor, Bob Smylie; and from Father Bob Bonnot, with whom I worked in television but whom I most admire as a dedicated Catholic priest for some forty years.

Anne Trudel, who worked with me on an earlier book, kept her eye on this one as well, jumping in with crucial suggestions about title, presentation, and resources.

And overseeing the entire endeavor was Robin Pippin, who always seemed to have a vision for this book, especially at those times when I felt uncertain.

I'm deeply indebted to each person named above and want to express my sincere gratitude.

Preface

Mention the word *novena*, and get ready for blank or, at best, curious looks. It's not a word that brings instant recognition nowadays.

Aging baby boomers with a Roman Catholic background, like me, will have some distant recollection. This is especially true if they spent at least part of their childhood in the early 1960s surrounded by and infused with a culture dominated by the pre–Vatican II church and the immigrant experience.

Still older Catholics will likely have more familiarity, perhaps vivid memories. Novenas happened frequently in parishes back then.

And Christians of other traditions might find the word mysterious.

Novenas can be defined most easily as prayers of devotion and intercession, offered for nine days in a row—or within another time period involving nine. They can be observed privately, or publicly in the church sanctuary, with a congregation present.

In the past, novenas were enormously popular because, in contrast to the central Roman Catholic liturgy of those days, the Latin Mass, novenas were accessible to everybody, with the words of the prayers, hymns, and sermons usually in the local language.

My mother often talked about novenas and, I suspect, prayed them. I'm guessing my grandmothers did also, at least the grandmother who was an Italian immigrant.

We heard of novenas dedicated to various "special intentions" announced from the pulpit fairly regularly. Two of the most popular were the novena to the Sacred Heart of Jesus, observed on the first Friday of each month, and a novena to the Blessed Virgin Mary, on the first Saturday.

I must say, though, that even as a kid who loved the tradition and ritual of the church, I cannot remember ever participating in a novena.

The idea of a novena slipped from my awareness, and almost from my memory, for decades. During the past three or four years, it has returned, especially in the context of war, following the September 11, 2001, terrorist attacks.

As the months passed and the death toll rose, I began to feel strongly moved to write about war, partially to explore my own feelings but also because for a very long time there seemed to be a shortage of soul-searching.

With no military draft, no rationing, no tax hikes, no pictures of the caskets of GIs returning home, and a deliberate decision by the U.S. government not to tabulate the Iraqi dead, I suppose an American can move through the daily routines of modern life without thinking much about Iraq or war or the 160,000 U.S. soldiers and Marines who, in early 2007, were serving there.

Or about the 27 million Iraqis who are hosting a conflict that has killed God only knows how many of them but which even conservative estimates place, at the time of this writing, at more than 100,000.

Maybe it's still possible for an American to avoid thinking about all that. Getting harder every day but still possible.

But can a Christian opt out? In a time of war—especially in time of war—isn't soul-searching the least one can do?

It was in this context that I began thinking that a deliberate process of discernment, divided into nine parts, structured as a kind of novena, seemed worth pursuing.

So please consider this *Novena in Time of War*. It's a book mostly of questions, not answers. A collection of explorations, not conclusions.

These are issues of deep personal struggle. My position may be different from yours. Mine could be wrong!

What's most important is to consider everything deeply and prayerfully, and, if necessary, to unlearn some ideas that we have "known" for so long that we've stopped thinking about them, about whether or not they're true.

I would like to confront some questions that might be answered differently by people with another lens of nationality, faith, or geography.

I'd also like to be so presumptuous as to try to figure out, by references to scripture and tradition, how God might evaluate the issue and, because of my own faith, what Jesus might say or do.

How to Use This Book

This book can be completed in nine days, although a better plan would be to spend nine weeks working through it with a Sunday school class or other small group, to allow time for discussion and contemplation.

Each of the nine chapters ends with a prayer, a suggested prayer focus to pursue until the reader begins the next chapter, and a list of questions for discussion and/or meditation.

A collateral benefit of researching this book has been a deeper understanding of the tradition of novena. I've learned that the number nine has rarely been a favored number. Throughout history, that status has belonged to the numbers three, seven, ten, and twelve. But nine was unlikely to be anybody's favorite.

To the ancient Greeks and Romans, nine was the number of days of official mourning for the dead.

In the fourth century, Saint Jerome wrote that "the number nine in Holy Writ is indicative of suffering and grief," which makes it a lot like war itself.

Roman Catholics, through their novenas, did their best to rehabilitate the reputation of the number nine, pointing out that Jesus remained in Mary's womb for nine months, and that the apostles stayed locked up in prayer for the nine days between the ascension of Jesus and the descent of the Holy Spirit on Pentecost (Acts 1:2-14).

In fact, some Catholic historians say the apostles, although they didn't know it, practiced the first novena in Christian history during that 216-hour period in Jerusalem.

Novena in Time of War is not a novena in the strict Roman Catholic tradition. It's a process, a course of study, prayer, reflection, and discussion—divided into nine parts.

However, it does share at least one significant similarity. Traditional novenas truly acknowledged and celebrated the power of prayer, especially focused, insistent, repetitive, intercessory prayer as demonstrated scripturally in Jesus' parable of the persistent widow (Luke 18:1-7) or Saint Paul's encouragement to "pray without ceasing" (1 Thess. 5:17).

Of all the plagues of humankind, war seems particularly worthy of our constant prayer. May we all pursue this novena in that spirit.

Chapter 1

THE ANCIENT CURSE

War may sometimes be a necessary evil. But no matter
how necessary, it is always an evil, never a good. We will
not learn how to live together in peace by killing each
other's children.

—Jimmy Carter, 39th President of the United States

ON THE first weekend of spring 2003, I find myself fixated
on a word I haven't thought much about in years. The word
is *genie*. You know, that spirit that suddenly comes out of a
bottle and sometimes takes human form.

This weekend, the genie on my mind, the genie out of
the bottle, is war.

War is an ancient genie. Often it seems distant, a strange
force from the far reaches of history—the Greeks and the
Trojans, Genghis Khan, Antietam, Stalingrad, Khe Sanh.

Then it becomes as real as today's news, an ancient genie
but young and vigorous as tomorrow, just awaiting its next
chance, released from its bottle, unleashing all the violence,
suspicion, and death it has always brought.

A genie from deepest history, and still ageless.

On the fourth day after the invasion of Iraq, a U.S. military unit, the 507th Maintenance Company, took a wrong turn near Nasiriyah and drove into an attack by Iraqi military forces. According to U.S. Army reports, eleven soldiers were killed, nine wounded, and seven others taken prisoner.

What catches my attention most this weekend is the follow-up report on the Arab television service Al Jazeera. U.S. prisoners of war, including a woman soldier, are seen being interviewed about why they're in Iraq.

Most disturbing are the bodies seen on video, some with head wounds. U.S. military officials are quoted as asking if the GIs might have been executed, a horrendous violation of the Geneva Conventions.

I speak with a colleague a little later. He's a dedicated opponent of the decision to invade Iraq. Yet he says the news about the possible executions makes him mad, makes him want to hurt the Iraqis, makes him feel the need for revenge.

I feel a swirl of emotions on this day:

- depression that we're once again in a war cycle,
- worry about the U.S. POWs,
- sympathy for the families of the dead soldiers,
- anger at myself for finding it easier to care about the casualties from my own nation,
- revulsion at the possibility that captured GIs have been executed,
- annoyance at the news media for treating war like a video game in which we act shocked that soldiers on

the other side—whose country has been attacked and invaded—might be so arrogant as to shoot back.

The genie is out of the bottle again, smiling at another opportunity. This genie has provoked and witnessed similar scenes millions of times for thousands of years.

The genie knows the cycle so well: the fear, the tribalism, the argument, the threat, the ultimatum, the attack, the violent response, the need to avenge the victims of the attack.

Or is it the victims of the violent response who must be avenged?

The fog of war obscures almost everything, evoking a sense of godlessness in all of this mess. I know that in fact God is present in the midst of it. And on some level of my being, I believe that God is in control and that, as I once heard Presbyterian minister Scott Black Johnston say, "God never loses a grip on us, on any of us."

Today, however, the genie appears to have the upper hand. Perhaps that's why I'm feeling so tired. But I bet the genie's feeling great, glad to be back in business again.

Prayer

Almighty God, someway, somehow, help us fix our minds and hearts to see the world as you see it, to see ourselves as you see us, and to see the men and women, the soldiers and families across the line of combat as you see them. Then nudge us in the direction you would have us take. Amen.

Prayer Focus

Picture a prisoner of war being held by your nation's military, and ask God how to pray for that prisoner.

Questions for Reflection

1. How does prayer change in time of war, and what do we say to God when our own nation's sons and daughters are "in combat"?

2. How do we understand who is the "enemy" in time of war?

3. Jesus never promised that we wouldn't have enemies—he surely had them! But he did give some challenging advice on how to deal with enemies: love them. In time of war, how does that advice challenge you?

Chapter 2

Us versus Them

I believe that my God is not just the God of the United
States—he is the God of the world. He does not just
love those who claim citizenship in these United States;
he loves all of humanity.

—**Dr. Ayodele Thomas**
Assistant Dean, Stanford University

A WORK ASSIGNMENT brought me to North Carolina on
the first Friday in May 2003. It was the same weekend that
newspapers around the world ran the photograph of President
Bush, in fighter pilot attire, on the deck of the aircraft
carrier USS *Abraham Lincoln*, off the coast of San Diego, a
large banner behind him reading "Mission Accomplished."

So, does this mean the war is over? The GIs will soon be
home? Will this war be even shorter than the 1991 Persian Gulf
conflict, and with even fewer Americans dead? All that would
be positive news, although the speeches and the stagecraft
disturbed me. On the flight from New York to North Carolina, I found myself, in thought at least, resembling the Pharisee in Luke 18:9-14, comforting myself that I am the kind of
American who takes war seriously, and who would never gloat

about a perceived victory. By the time we landed, I had worked myself into quite a tizzy.

By coincidence, or perhaps as evidence of God's sense of humor, that very night I would have my self-righteous balloon burst during a visit with our friends Elizabeth and Peter Storey.

Peter spent many years as a Methodist pastor and bishop in South Africa. He struggled publicly, and at great personal peril, against the racial segregation known as apartheid. Peter later served as interim pastor of Calvary United Methodist Church in Nashville, where our family once held membership.

For about seven years after Peter's retirement, he and Elizabeth lived in the United States each spring, and Peter taught at Duke Divinity School. Our conversation on that beautiful spring evening centered on the war in Iraq, which had begun six weeks earlier.

Over a Caesar salad, bread, iced tea, coffee, and dessert, Elizabeth, Peter, and I discussed the events of the past three months, including the huge public demonstrations that occurred in many cities around the world on February 15, 2003, with an estimated 11 million people marching in opposition to what was seen, accurately as it turned out, as the impending war in Iraq.

In the course of the discussion, I mentioned that many of the Americans who either participated in those demonstrations, or at least supported their aim, now felt obligated to back the troops, overseas and under fire, and were tempering their uneasiness about the war.

I believe I may have put forth the observation that many U.S. citizens wanted to, in the traditional phrase, "support our boys."

Peter's response was short, direct, and withering:

"Those boys are over there killing people."

The words sting. And I feel it personally. Once upon a time I was one of "those boys" serving in the U.S. military overseas in a combat zone during a war.

I never thought of myself as "killing people."

But that's what happens in war. That's what always has happened. Our "boys" (and "girls") are killing people and, although it was not as evident in May 2003 as it became later, Americans are also being killed.

As I pondered Peter's words in the days that followed, I wondered a lot about past wars and that whole idea of how we support our troops.

Did German families feel obligated to support their troops during the invasion of Poland in the first half of September 1939?

Did South Africans rally around their sons, in the military uniform of their nation, as they enforced apartheid?

I bet they did. War is the best friend tribalism ever had.

And if in war, truth is the first casualty, then our sense of common humanity, the reality of the human family, is surely the second.

Peter Storey has addressed that subject too, with what sounds to my ears like the definitive rebuke of the tribalism that so often leads to and facilitates war.

"For Christians, if we accept that Christ has bound us to our neighbor, every war is a civil war, and even more than that, if God is the parent of us all, every war is a form of fratricide," Storey wrote in February 2007.

And yet, Peter's seven-word response to me in May 2003 has resonated most powerfully, made me think long and deeply.

"Those boys are over there killing people."

A simple statement about all armies, all insurgents, all guerrillas, all combatants, all terrorists, in all wars. A statement that doesn't necessarily mean, I suppose, that there would never be a justification for war.

Our "boys" were killing people on D-Day, June 6, 1944. And they continued to kill people as they moved through Western Europe for the next eleven months and liberated Hitler's concentration camps.

We wince, of course, at referring to the activities of members of "the greatest generation" that way. They were fighting to destroy Nazi power and, to this day, it's difficult for me to question that struggle.

So we use different vocabulary. And we extend the benefit of the doubt to the soldiers fighting on our side, "our boys."

That's how it is in war, how it always has been. And it's easy to mix in history, culture, flags, and anthems until our vision gets awfully clouded.

We Americans need to at least consider the perspective of a citizen of another nation—in this case, Peter Storey—and hear his words on the essential nature of all war.

"Those boys are over there killing people."

Uncomfortable words to hear.

But when it comes to something as monumental as war, our discomfort is not the worst thing. Not even close.

Prayer

Almighty God, the story line of war is ancient and unchanged. In our view, it's always about "us" and "them." But in your eyes, "us" and "them" are all yours, your children. Help us to rewrite the tired old lines that lead to death and to move closer to you and your perspective. Amen.

Prayer Focus

Picture in your mind a person unlike you—a person on the "other" side who is Arab, Muslim, living in Iraq. Tell yourself that this person is a member of your family. Then pray that God will move in your life until you believe it.

Questions for Reflection

1. How does patriotism affect our faith in wartime? How can we ensure that love for our country doesn't cause us to conclude that ours is the more worthy nation in God's sight, that God is on our side?

2. A popular maxim, attributed to former U.S. Senator Arthur Vandenberg, says, "Politics stops at the water's edge." The idea is that Americans should be united on

foreign policy—that they shouldn't question a war when the nation's military personnel are in battle. How do you react to the idea of closing off debate and remaining silent because a war is under way?

3. How can persons of faith pray in a situation in which they are not certain that their country is morally and ethically right in its pursuit of war? As an American, can you imagine such a situation?

Chapter 3

SHALOM IN THE ORDINARY

They shall beat their swords into plowshares,
and their spears into pruning hooks.

—Isaiah 2:4

HOW ARE a woman in Charleston, South Carolina, who collects thread, and a minister in Harrisburg, Pennsylvania, who serves as a military chaplain, connected to a book of meditations on war?

Well, you be the judge.

I met Terry Helwig in May 2004, about three years after she had begun The Thread Project: One World, One Cloth.

Her idea was to collect thread from people all over the world and tie, sew, or otherwise connect that thread in a series of huge tapestries that would represent a beautiful kind of unity in diversity.

"The idea seemed to find me," Terry recalled, "but I couldn't figure out the how or the why of it, and I just dismissed the idea.

"Then, after the night of September 11, I was despairing, like many people around the world.

"And that's when I went to bed thinking that the world is hanging by a thread. Then I thought, *Maybe it's enough to be hanging by a thread, if we all pull together and do our one little piece.*"

Terry began publicizing her idea through an Internet Web site and, by the time I first met her, had received thread from more than thirty countries, much of it accompanied by deeply personal stories.

Fabric from the "killing fields" of Cambodia, where 1.7 million people died.

A strip of cloth designed by a group of Zulu women in Africa.

A thread from the blanket of a dead child, donated by a grieving mother.

By May 2004, Terry Helwig had collected enough thread and had enlisted the help of enough weavers to create two four-teen-by-seven-foot cloths. Her goal was to complete five more cloths and eventually display all seven at the United Nations.

Fast-forward more than two years to August 2006, to Harrisburg, Pennsylvania, home of Pastor Richard Denison and members of his congregation at Paxton United Methodist Church.

Rick Denison serves as a chaplain for the Air National Guard 193rd Special Operations Wing. The pastor has been mobilized to active duty and shipped overseas twice, to Afghanistan in 2002 and to Iraq in 2004.

One day, while he was accompanying U.S. troops to a small village north of Baghdad so they could distribute clothing to Iraqi kids, a young girl came up to Denison and asked if he had any dresses.

He didn't. But that night the pastor sent an e-mail to the women of his congregation back in Harrisburg, along with some digital photos of the dresses young Iraqi girls wear. Soon the women designed patterns, cut out material, sewed it together, and shipped twenty-five dresses.

Their reputation spread to an Iraqi school for girls. Soon a request for *nine hundred* dresses came to Paxton UMC. The women responded by setting up a virtual dress factory at the church every Thursday. When I met them, they had already sent five hundred dresses to Iraq.

In a time of seemingly endless war—with daily roadside bombings, thousands of Iraqi civilians dead, more than three thousand GIs already killed, and U.S. troops so often targeted as occupiers—I find much to embrace in this story of a small group of American women making dresses for Iraqi girls.

It's significant that they didn't simply ship over store-bought dresses. They recognized that American cultural norms would offend the mostly Arab, mostly Muslim girls in Iraq. The women showed respect for local custom by referring to photos of Iraqi clothing styles and by producing similar dresses.

Pastor Rick Denison saw the gift as more than just clothing. "I think it's really important, because so much death and destruction occur over in Iraq. This was a very people-to-people way of showing that someone in America cares.

"The first time I visited a village there, I had cameras and we were taking pictures, and every mother wanted us to take a picture of all her children gathered around her. And I realized that people in every country are the same: everybody's proud of their children."

I found being with Rick Denison both humbling and encouraging. This is a man who has already served two tours of duty in very dangerous places, walked around for months wearing forty pounds of body armor, and injured his knee while running into a bunker during a bomb attack.

He serves as a pastor, shepherd, and counselor to troops far from their families, living in constant danger of imminent death. He's an American, a military officer, and a Christian— three identities not always warmly embraced in southwest Asia.

And now that he's back in the States, he's offering the people of his congregation a message that, in a time of war, is both comforting and challenging.

"The thing that struck me was that every week someone in church requests prayer for our service people who are overseas," Denison said. "I think that's important, but it hit me that God will not honor our prayer for service people until we also pray for the people of Iraq and, at the same time, pray for the terrorists as well."

Terry Helwig's idea of creating tapestries using thread from across the world, conceived in the pain of the night of September 11, 2001, has now come full circle.

On the fifth anniversary of the terrorist attacks, all seven tapestries hung in public display at St. Paul's Chapel in Lower Manhattan, across the street from Ground Zero. More than fifty thousand people from seventy countries participated in the project.

"We're in a global community. And I think, with regard to rugged individualism, we need to look at alternatives," Terry reflected.

The stories of Terry Helwig and Rick Denison share a central detail: the universality of thread. In all nations, in all cultures, we clothe ourselves and our children using thread, just as we all feed ourselves with bread, another universal gift of God.

And, as Terry and Rick learned independently of each other, we all want to stand together with our families, and we want to share our stories.

In my introspective, sometimes crazier moments, the incidents described in these stories seem to offer an antidote for the ancient disease of war.

PRAYER

O High and Lofty One who inhabits eternity, who sees backward and forward from our brief lives and far beyond our small communities, help us to notice your many simple but essential gifts that all your children share in common—thread, bread, water, family—and challenge us to build on those similarities when we are tempted to fight over our differences. Amen.

Prayer Focus

Picture a mother whose adult child has died after setting a roadside bomb that killed U.S. troops. Ask God to help you to pray for her, for she also has suffered a terrible loss.

Questions for Reflection

1. One of the women making the dresses for the Iraqi girls expressed the hope that this gift would change the negative attitudes of Iraqis toward Americans. Discuss how Iraqis might have come to embrace such attitudes. Then talk about how we Americans have come to embrace our attitudes toward Iraqis. What needs to change in the thinking of both sides?

2. How do you feel about Pastor Denison's insistence that we pray not only for our own troops overseas but also for the Iraqi people and the terrorists?

3. How would you compose a prayer for the terrorists, or is that simply impossible for you at this point?

Chapter 4

REMEMBERING THE FALLEN

War would end if the dead could return.

—Stanley Baldwin
Twentieth-century British prime minister

ON THE NIGHT in September 2004 when the U.S. military death toll in Iraq reached one thousand, I happened to be in Cincinnati on a business trip.

I had read in various e-mails about candlelight vigils being held across the nation. For a variety of reasons—curiosity, guilty conscience, the need to get out of the hotel room for a while—I walked through downtown Cincinnati to see if I might, by happenstance, encounter a vigil.

I didn't find one, but since I don't know my way around Cincinnati very well, my inability to locate a vigil means nothing. I feel pretty sure that somewhere in that city, the sad milestone was being memorialized.

Like virtually everything about the war in Iraq, the issue of U.S. casualties makes me very uncomfortable. I feel deep sadness when I stare at the names, the hometowns, the branches of service, and the ages of the U.S. military dead. My limited military experience, with one admittedly brief exposure to war, does give me some insight into those Americans who serve in the military—I've known them as friends and comrades—and it's easy for me to form a mental picture, not always completely accurate, of course, but real.

Now that I'm a middle-aged father with two of three sons in their twenties, I read the ages of the dead, and it dawns on me that many of these soldiers are younger than my two older children.

And I think of how these now-dead young people likely played with Transformers toys and watched *Sesame Street* and *Back to the Future* movies countless times as kids, just as my sons did. They're gone, some before their twenty-fifth birthday.

Then I realize that I'm focusing on the U.S. dead, feeling their loss acutely and neglecting to think of the Iraqi dead—other people's children—with the same depth of sorrow.

Maybe it's impossible to feel the pain of the "other side" as deeply as we grieve our own losses. Perhaps we humans are hardwired to be tribal. Yet something about that feels wrong.

Shouldn't Christianity make us counterintuitive? Jesus was.

What also feels wrong is how easy it is to think only occasionally about the deaths in Iraq.

As one who remembers the Vietnam War well—although primarily from the safe vantage point of junior high and high school—and who was exposed to the draft (with a high lottery number) only in the final year of conscription in the United States, I wonder why we Americans seem to be handling this war so well, as the years pass and the death toll mounts.

It seems to be taking a long time for the private angst, which so many confess, to become public anger—or, if not anger, at least grief.

It's not that the war is ignored. Virtually since the start of combat in March 2003, there have been debates in the op-ed pages and frequent video reports on television.

The war played a major role in the 2004 and 2006 elections, although with opposite results. And certain milestones in the war, such as the anniversary of its beginning, have been marked by large rallies and marches. But unlike the intense feeling of, say, 1968, it all feels quite manageable.

The death toll, even if we—God forgive us—concentrate only on the number of Americans killed, has not sent thousands of people repeatedly into the streets. Sometimes it seems as though the only place to find intense focus on the war dead is the Internet, where many memorial Web sites operate.

I know that the toll in Vietnam was dramatically higher. I can recall, when I was a junior-high student, the now-defunct *Evening Bulletin* in Philadelphia running a summary of the war every Saturday. I remember often reading that 250 or 300 U.S. troops had been killed that week. Those numbers do not reflect the worst weeks!

In the deadliest year of the war, 1968, almost 15,000 Americans died—more than a quarter of the war's total of 58,193. Estimates of the Vietnamese dead, military and civilian, range between 2 and 5 *million*.

Thank God, the deaths in Iraq have not been on a level with Vietnam—yet. That must seem like a callous statement to the families, Iraqi and American, whose sons, daughters, husbands, fathers, wives, and mothers are not coming home.

Certainly, the times and the wars are very different, and those differences may reveal some reasons for the lower level of engagement by the public and by communities of faith.

Like the fact that there's no longer a military draft, which would make the consequence of this war real to a larger segment of the population.

Or the recognition that our too-busy society stays distracted by its seemingly endless "entertainment culture."

Or the thought that many people reluctantly believe that war is necessary and unavoidable in the wake of 9/11. I suspect this was especially true in the first couple of years after the invasion of Iraq in 2003.

And I can accept that reasonable and faithful people can support war in some circumstances. For most of my life, I have fallen into that category and still can imagine a few situations where my growing pacifism might reach its limit.

After reading Harrison Salisbury's book *The 900 Days: The Siege of Leningrad*, I realized that if I had lived on the outskirts of Leningrad in September 1941, I would have joined in firing a mortar or a rifle at Hitler's advancing army.

What bothers me most is not that many Americans still support the war, or that others find themselves morally conflicted about it, pulled in several different directions. That's okay. Struggling with the issue is a good thing.

I guess I'd just like to know that we're all thinking about it, every day, and treating it urgently. Because it is urgent.

Prayer

Creator of the universe, comfort the families whose sons and daughters, husbands and wives have been killed in the current war. Guide our political leaders to be humble, discerning, and constantly aware of the personal sacrifices resulting from our policies. Help us to examine all our statements and actions and never to assume that our perspective, or that of our nation, is beyond challenge. Amen.

Prayer Focus

Picture a soldier serving in your country's military who has lost a limb or is otherwise permanently disabled from war wounds. Ask God how to pray for that person, and then do it.

Questions for Reflection

1. How do you react to the idea that an "age of terrorism" means maintaining the nation on a "war footing" for years or even decades?

2. We tend to feel the deaths of the women and men in our own nation's forces more acutely than losses on the other side. As a Christian, how difficult is it for you to pray for people, including soldiers, on the "other" side during a war?

3. Occasionally we hear reports from other countries in which people charge that the United States is also "terrorist,"

pointing to the awesome power this country can bring against much weaker nations. How do you react when you hear that charge? Even if you don't believe it's true, discuss how a person living elsewhere might embrace that view.

Chapter 5

AN INSTINCT FOR LIFE

You recognize you did the unthinkable. You blasted
away a piece of yourself, violated some trust with God.

—**Stewart Brown**
Boulder Vet Center, Boulder, Colorado

WHAT COULD be worse than going to war, fighting in
house-to-house urban combat, driving through streets where
homemade bombs explode, seeing your comrades and innocent civilians blown to bits, and then losing your own arm
or leg?

What could be worse?

Killing a soldier fighting for the other side.

Hard to believe? I would have doubted it too, until I read
a story in the *New Yorker* magazine in July 2004.

The reporter, Dan Baum, writes of a visit with soldiers
grievously wounded in Iraq—amputees—at Walter Reed
Army Medical Center.

Baum says he was struck by how easily the soldiers could
talk, even occasionally joke, about the horrible incidents that
left them with their legs or arms blown off.

That is, until the conversation shifted to the killing they had done. Then the words did not come as easily; "a pall would settle over them," Baum wrote.

The congressionally funded National Vietnam Veterans Readjustment Study included interviews with almost seventeen hundred men who had served in Vietnam. If a soldier believed he had killed in combat, he was more likely to suffer from post-traumatic stress disorder.

Even during World War II, still considered by most Americans to be the quintessential "just war," field commanders reported difficulty in getting their troops to shoot at enemy soldiers. Soldiers had to be rigorously trained to do it. By the time of the Vietnam War, that training had apparently worked so well that an estimated 90 percent of U.S. soldiers were firing their weapons.

War tends to make us think tribally. People who feel surrounded by danger—whose lives could end violently at any moment—might be excused for becoming primal in their desire to protect themselves and their comrades.

Yet even with that "justification," the studies suggest that we humans don't easily kill other people, even if those people are trying to kill us. It's almost as though, deep down, we know we're all related, as children of God.

Somewhere in its first section, usually within the first five to six pages, the *New York Times* prints the names of U.S. military personnel killed in the Iraq war each day.

As I sit or stand on the subway, reading the paper, I try to spend time with each name. I read the rank, the name, the hometown, the age—especially the age.

I try hard to separate politics from people when it comes to this sad ritual. I want to pray daily for the people whose names I read in the newspaper. And for their families who must move on without them.

And for the Iraqis. Depending on what sources you check, the death rate of Iraqis compared with that of U.S. military personnel is at least twenty to one.

And, theoretically at least, for every soldier whose life ends, another lives with the knowledge of having killed.

For many months, even years, Americans back home have had the luxury not to think much about this war—unless they choose to.

When they do think about it, likely they think first of the dead—the American dead. And then of the soldiers who have returned with catastrophic wounds.

Let's also remember those who return physically unscathed. They have their bodies and their health. But the odds are, they still have been terribly wounded.

PRAYER

Almighty God, Psalm 139 says we are all wonderfully made by you. You created us with a core humanity that apparently survives, even in the midst of horrible violence. Let us celebrate this natural instinct to preserve life, and deeply ponder it, especially at those times when war seems so attractive, or inevitable. Amen.

Prayer Focus

Picture a soldier serving in your nation's military who has killed in the war. Ask God how to pray for that soldier, and then do it.

Questions for Reflection

1. Does the survey referred to in this meditation surprise you? Why or why not? Why do you think that men and women apparently have difficulty taking another's life, even in the midst of war?

2. Do you think this reluctance to kill is unique to American troops, or is it realistic to think that nations can build on that natural tendency in order to lessen the frequency of war?

3. Military officers have said that troops must be "taught" to fire instinctively, since the natural instinct is not to kill. Is it possible that the tribalism so common in war, the notion that the life of the person on the other side is "cheaper" and not as important as the life of the person on our side, must also be taught, in order to overcome natural instinct?

Chapter 6

War Changes Things— and People

> What does the LORD require of you
> but to do justice, and to love kindness,
> and to walk humbly with your God?
>
> —Micah 6:8

A NOVENA COULD BE considered a nine-act play moving toward, if not a climax, at least a new place. A journey in which we grow or become otherwise transformed.

Ideally, that journey is one of discernment or discovery, spiritually and socially—in this case, during a time of war.

A journey fueled by the power of prayer.

A sojourn that may not be easy.

I am a U.S. Navy veteran who served as an enlisted man on active duty in a combat zone during the relatively brief 1991 Gulf War.

I was not one of the "shooters," the slang term for those directly involved in combat operations, but rather one of the many more service members who serve in a logistical or support role. Dodging errant Scud missiles, including the one that did hit a target and killed twenty-nine Americans, was probably as close as I came to physical danger.

Although my father, the son of Italian immigrants, served three years as a draftee in the U.S. Army Air Corps during World War II, arriving in the European Theater in February 1944, under fire at Naples, we weren't what would be called a military family. My parents never encouraged military service.

But being so close to the immigrant experience, and being Catholic, and having parents who were the products of blue-collar culture, I grew up with a sense that American young men have a duty to serve, including military service, if circumstances call for it. You might disagree with the politics of a war, and you had a right to speak out and to vote.

And, as Catholics, at least as I understood it, we had no problem with conscientious objectors. Our faith taught that we should understand and respect persons whose deep moral opposition to war required them to decline service.

But there was also that idea of duty. Otherwise, the next guy would have to go in your place, and for that to happen was unacceptable.

I had no interest in waging war, carrying a weapon (which I have done only occasionally), or firing a weapon in combat (which I have never done).

To me, being in the military came down to three values: service, sacrifice, and experience. Later, and I know this sounds strange, I developed a political reason.

As a young adult, I enlisted in the Naval Reserve primarily because I realized that, in the United States, men of my age, education, and income are never required, or even expected, to serve in the military, and that bothered me. It seemed elitist, and I didn't want to be part of that.

However, my brief active military service in the Persian Gulf in 1991 did introduce me to certain realities of war, especially their effects on people, that I suspect I never would have understood without the experience.

I recently looked through a diary I kept from that period and reviewed some entries.

First, there's the recognition of death, both military and civilian, as a regular by-product of war. I recall waking up from a nap as our plane flew toward the war zone, looking at my dog tags, and noting that the information on them included my blood type and religious preference. I thought, *The blood type is there if a doctor is trying to save my life, and the religious preference is there if she can't!*

I mentioned to a colleague back in the States that in war, the other guy is trying to kill you, but it's nothing personal, just part of the job. At the time, I thought my attitude was tough and realistic. But today, more than sixteen years later, I'm struck by the insanity of it.

A lot of little incidents reveal the effect war can have on us.

In January 1991 a bunch of us were listening to a story on the radio reporting that a Saudi fighter pilot had shot down two Iraqi planes on one mission. I remember how one of my American comrades reacted: "G.D., think how many our guys will get." Perhaps that was just old-fashioned and, ultimately, harmless cheerleading, similar to what we see during the Olympics.

But it also demonstrates the chauvinism of the powerful toward the less powerful that can arise so quickly among members of a large expeditionary force. From there it's a short step to resentment on the part of folks we are supposed to be helping.

I recall a few conversations that included the word *raghead* and the phrase "smoke an Arab"; these discussions showed me that tribalism seems to come more easily during war. Such tribalism managed to survive even during the Gulf War, where the United States was part of a coalition of more than thirty nations, including several which are predominantly Arab.

The violence of war can definitely dehumanize us.

We spent one day traveling along the road that runs through Saudi Arabia and into Kuwait, after the ground forces had passed on their way north to Kuwait City. Bombed and burned trucks and tanks littered the desert, with oil fires visible on the horizon. A young sergeant announced loudly to our group that he wanted to see a "dead body, take a picture, and show it to his father" back home.

There is nothing comprehensive or scientific about any of my recollections—they prove nothing. But neither are they meaningless, even though such incidents pale in comparison with, for example, videotaped beheadings of prisoners, as we've seen in the Iraq War.

Such incidents remind us how war can change us. When

we hear or read about alleged mistreatment, torture, or atrocities—no matter which side is accused—it's wise not to spring to a quick defense or denial. These things happen, and always have happened, in war.

And being American and serving under the U.S. flag don't provide an inoculation. Here's another reason to pray daily for troops in the war zone, because physical danger is not the only peril they face.

Nonetheless, in my own limited experience, I found the official policy of the U.S. military during the Persian Gulf War, and the attitude and behavior of a majority of our officers, to be extremely sensitive to local customs.

One directive I recall vividly came before the start of Ramadan, in which we were instructed not to appear on the street during daylight hours drinking anything, not even a bottle of water, or eating anything, including chewing gum, out of respect for Muslim religious observance.

So when it comes to generic bashing of the U.S. military, don't come to me. That's not my thing. I knew and served with too many decent people.

Now I am firmly ensconced in middle age, with our two older sons already adults, and with men and women their age serving and dying overseas.

Whether it's the paternal instinct of an aging man or a growing conviction of the insanity of what war does to God's children in all countries, I don't know. But no matter what the uniform worn or the language spoken or the faith professed, I'm tired of people dying.

Prayer

God of the universe, who considers every person on earth your child, we confess that we have ignored the ancient scriptural instruction to do justice, love kindness, and, especially, to walk humbly. Guide us as we seek a gentler and more respectful path, to retain the passion to right the wrongs we see, as Zechariah tells us, "not by might, nor by power" but by your spirit living in us. Amen.

Prayer Focus

Picture a soldier who is totally committed to military service, who believes the war is right, and who would disagree with your doubts. Ask God how to pray for that soldier and how to pray for yourself.

Questions for Reflection

1. Many men and women join the military not because of a desire to participate in war but out of a sense of duty to serve or because of perceived economic necessity. One point of view would maintain that all of them are equally complicit in the violence of war. What do you think about that view?

2. What are some legitimate reasons for a nation to resort to war as a means of stopping or reversing an action it

considers wrong? For example, is war justified to oust the invader of a sovereign country? Is it justified to dismantle concentration camps? Is it justified to stop a government-sponsored policy of ethnic cleansing? Where do you draw the line against war as a response?

3. What are the moral and ethical implications of a country maintaining a military force but exempting most citizens from the obligation to serve?

Chapter 7

OTHER PEOPLE'S NEIGHBORHOOD

How much devastation are we permitted to visit on other people in order to keep the land of the free, free from terrorists?

—Gordon D. Marino, St. Olaf College

PRESIDENT GEORGE W. BUSH addressed the graduating class at the U.S. Naval Academy in Annapolis in 2005 with a speech that included the following sentence:

"We are taking the fight to the enemy abroad so we do not have to face them here at home."

In many interviews I have seen with U.S. military personnel—some in their early twenties with a couple of babies or toddlers at home—the interviewees have said much the same thing, sincerely telling reporters that they're serving in Iraq so their children, their families "don't have to face this at home."

September 11, 2001 profoundly shook all of us who live in the United States.

Approximately three thousand people were killed in less than two hours, by acts of premeditated murder.

Hardest of all to process was the idea of that horror happening in our country, within our seemingly secure borders, in our nation's capital, in the streets of our largest city, and in a field in rural Pennsylvania.

Hardest because we felt we have a right, an expectation, to be safe in our communities.

I live in New York City. I doubt that I will ever live long enough to forget every detail of that Tuesday and the months that followed.

Walking uptown at noon in bright sunshine with thousands of shaken people, many of them covered with ash and debris.

Watching military convoys move downtown past the elegant apartments of Park Avenue in the gathering twilight, headed for an armory that is usually used for art shows.

Smelling the stench in the air, a combination of God only knows what, breathed by those of us who live or work in Lower Manhattan, as fires burned underground for months.

Seeing crowds of people on church steps, leaving the funerals of firefighters for weeks through that autumn.

I have made it a habit of praying daily that not only my community—but no community—ever has to go through that again. I don't doubt that many of the soldiers and Marines who enlisted in the wake of 9/11 did so with the same motivation.

A journalist friend who traveled with soldiers deployed to the Middle East told me their plane flew right over Ground Zero , and an officer advised the troops to look down on the wreckage as a reminder of why they were shipping out.

Having said all that, I confess to being disturbed about the idea that we "fight them there so we don't have to fight them here." We want to keep death and destruction out of our neighborhoods, but it's okay for that to happen in someone else's neighborhood?

As disciples of Jesus, we belong to a worldwide community dedicated to a movement that transcends all national borders. We should never forget that there are other people living "over there" besides insurgents, suicidal terrorists, and roadside bombers. Mothers. Children. Teachers. Grocers. Barbers. Senior citizens.

Perhaps the Iraqis feel, as we do about ourselves, that they have a right to be safe in their communities.

As one who lives in a city that is always a target—a community that lost 2,750 people on September 11, 40 percent of whom vanished without a trace—I realize this is difficult territory to explore.

I'm sensitive to the argument that "they hit us first," and we're retaliating in legitimate self-defense. And I agree, reluctantly, that there are times when force may be necessary to apprehend criminal suspects and remove sanctuaries for terrorists, such as Taliban-controlled Afghanistan in 2001. Sometimes force is required in order to prevent greater violence and more widespread suffering and death.

But war is such a monumental step, such a deadly enterprise, that people of faith must never stop asking questions, evaluating policies, challenging assumptions.

Is it better to "fight them there so we don't have to fight

them here"? Better for us, for sure. If you and your family lived "there," however, would you still agree?

I'm thankful to God that we have, to date, not experienced another major terrorist attack on U.S. soil since September 11, 2001. But I think it's fair to raise the question of whether or not we're being arrogant and self-serving when we agree that it's better to allow another community of God's children to host a war so we don't have to go through that pain ourselves.

PRAYER

Almighty God, from your vantage point, "there" and "here" have little meaning. We know that you were with us in the United States on that terrible Tuesday in September. And we know that you are also standing amid the people living through the horror of war, every day and every night, in the many communities where violence reigns around this globe. Help us to close our eyes and just imagine for a moment that *those* communities are *our* communities, because all of them are yours. Amen.

PRAYER FOCUS

Picture a teenage boy in a country where the military of your nation is operating, who resents the presence of your nation's soldiers and dreams of retribution. Ask God how to pray for that boy, and then do it.

QUESTIONS FOR REFLECTION

1. How do you feel about the morality of confronting an adversary, and waging war far away, and justifying it as a preferred alternative to doing the same in your own community?

2. What responsibility do we have to the people who live in the areas where we wage war, people whose lives are dramatically changed, if not ended, even though they have never harmed us?

3. Imagine that you are a citizen of a smaller country, with fewer resources and less power. How do you think you would feel about a major power deciding to wage war in your area to protect its own citizens from the effect of war at home?

Chapter 8

RIGHTEOUS, NOT SELF-RIGHTEOUS

From the arrogance that thinks it knows all truth
Good Lord, deliver [us].

—Kenyan Prayer

ASK FOLKS who live in New York City what time of year has the best weather, and they'll tell you September.

And so it was in mid-September 2006 that I found myself standing along the east side of Fifth Avenue, on a beautiful sunny Sunday, holding two simple poster boards. Each bore the name of an American who had died in the Iraq War.

One man served as a sergeant with a field artillery battalion. A father of four, he died at age forty-two, having worked as a school bus driver in a northeastern state before being mobilized with his reserve unit.

The other was a staff sergeant with the U.S. Marine Corps. A native of the American South, he had been living in California with his wife and two children before going to Iraq to serve as a helicopter crew chief.

When he was killed in a helicopter crash during the summer of 2004, the Marine was serving his second tour of duty. He was twenty-six, eight months older than our eldest son.

Any attempt to pray a novena in time of war must, first and foremost, confront the reality of the dead, the details of their lives and the void in their families left behind.

Nobody is more invested.

In fact, the reason I stood on the street across from Central Park that morning, accompanied by more than two thousand others, was an organized vigil called "Number the Dead."

The idea was to station people along Fifth Avenue from Eighth Street to Ninety-eighth Street, a distance of about four and a half miles, with signs displaying the names of the roughly 2,700 Americans killed, as of that date, since the start of the Iraq War. In each block, one person held an additional sign remembering the Iraqi dead, estimated at that time to be at least 43,000.

Number the Dead was organized by a young woman named Annie Lennon Carroll and some of her former film school classmates from New York University. In the interest of full disclosure, Annie and I once worked for the same television production company in Lower Manhattan.

Number the Dead was a silent, hourlong vigil from 10:00 until 11:00 a.m.

Its silent nature certainly appealed to me. But most powerful was its focus on the dead.

Whether a person supports the war, opposes it, or struggles with conflicting emotions about it, how could anyone disagree with the idea of a one-hour public focus on those who gave their lives?

It's beyond politics, right?

Yet I suppose there's no other way to describe our action except as an antiwar demonstration, because to deeply consider the human consequences of war, to name and "Number the Dead," will almost always cause a person to oppose war or at least regard it with the deepest misgivings.

And I know that many of the surviving family members of those whose names we displayed would not approve of our public action. In fact, although I wanted to identify in this book the American military service members whose names I displayed that morning, surviving family members did not allow it, and I am sensitive to their feelings.

So Christians, or any persons of faith or of no faith, who feel called to question a policy of war must also be willing to consider the feelings of those who have lost so much. Those folks who often find that their own faith, along with the grieving process, leads them to a different conclusion.

That's a good reason to spend at least some time on the many Web sites that operate as tributes to those who have died.

The mother of the Marine whose name I held up that morning said that she begged her youngest son not to join the Marines, but he enlisted two days after high school graduation. She said he believed strongly in the mission in Iraq.

"He wanted to be over there, to help those people secure their freedom," his older brother added.

There was a tradition of military service in his family—his grandfather was a Marine, and his father and older brother served in the Navy.

The reservist whose name I displayed, the one who worked

as a school bus driver until his unit was mobilized, "loved what he was doing and was proud to be serving his country."

One Web site tribute thanks that sergeant and "all the others that have given their lives so that others may be free."

Many who have served believe that they were struggling to preserve freedom for Americans or to secure freedom for the Iraqi people. I could never be so arrogant as to question the motives of those who have sacrificed everything.

And it's true that sometimes something positive can be identified as a result of a war, such as the removal of a brutal dictatorship, the reversal of an invasion, an end to "ethnic cleansing," or the liberation of a concentration camp.

But war brings with it such death, such destruction, such a contradiction of everything virtually every faith on earth teaches, that it's fair to ask the questions: Is there an alternative? Did we really try everything else for as long as possible? Does the "positive" really outweigh the terrible pain?

Even after war begins, must we always continue, or do we have other options, and are we exploring them?

Not only is it fair to raise those questions; asking them is really the least we can do.

That's our obligation. And as Christians or as people of any faith, we also share the responsibility to pray daily for those serving in the war zones—on both "sides"—and for their families, especially survivors of those who have been killed.

Our prayers need to include officials of our government. Even if we disagree with their policies. Even if we feel so angry or frustrated that praying for them feels almost impossible.

Even when others encourage us to ridicule them as part of our opposition.

We must remember the common humanity of all of us.

Reading back over this chapter, I realize that I sound very conflicted and ambivalent. I guess I am!

It's so important to not sound preachy and to maintain humanity and compassion when dealing with an issue that raises such powerful emotions.

So why am I—a military veteran who has never been accused of being overly demonstrative, emotionally or otherwise—standing on the street in a public demonstration, questioning my country's participation in a war?

In response to that question, I can only retreat to Jesus and my fumbling, clumsy attempts at being a disciple. I just don't find much evidence that Jesus would have ever endorsed a war, any war. I bet he'd tell us to go back, sit down, and find another way.

PRAYER

Almighty God, in the midst of the violence of war, help us to be gentle with one another, and ensure that our struggle for righteousness doesn't become self-righteous. Help us respect one another's pain, conscience, and our shared humanity. Let those of us who still possess the precious gift of life hold the dead of all wars in our hearts, as you hold them in your eternal care. Amen.

Prayer Focus

Pray for yourself that, no matter what your opinion or even deeply held belief happens to be regarding war, God will grant you the grace to be always both passionate and compassionate.

Questions for Reflection

1. What do you think of the idea that public demonstrations opposing a war give encouragement to those fighting on the other side?

2. Jesus' words in scripture have been claimed by pacifists who oppose all wars, by people opposing specific conflicts, and also by those who seek to justify war in certain circumstances:

    "Do not think that I have come to bring peace to the earth; I have not come to bring peace, but a sword." (Matthew 10:34)

    Read Matthew 10:32-42 for more context. How does your faith lead you to interpret Jesus' words?

3. How do you react to the argument that withdrawing from a war before a clear resolution means those who already lost their lives fighting on your nation's side have "died in vain"?

Chapter 9

HATING WAR, NOT WARRIORS

> What difference does it make to the dead, the orphans
> and the homeless, whether the mad destruction is
> wrought under the name of totalitarianism or the holy
> name of liberty or democracy?
>
> —Mahatma Gandhi
> **Indian political and spiritual leader (1869–1948)**

IMAGINE BEING a sixteen-year-old girl and seeing a foreign army invade your country.

Intelligence officers of that foreign army harass and detain your father. A few days later, that army herds you into an old school that has become a prison camp, where you live as a virtual captive for the next three years.

For the first six months, the army doesn't even feed you. Fortunately, your friends outside the walls bring food to your family each day.

Finally, after three years, your own country's military forces attack in an attempt to drive out the occupying army. A terrible battle goes on for days, a struggle that leaves your father dead and your mother so seriously wounded that doctors predict, incorrectly it turns out, that she will not survive.

How do you think you'd feel about that foreign army, whose actions robbed you of your freedom, your father, and practically your own life?

On a sunny, windy, and cool day late one April, I had the privilege of spending an hour or two learning more about that sixteen-year-old girl's story.

Frances-Helen Foley Guest, in her eighties now, is still vigorous. She, like my family and me, is a member of the Church of St. Paul and St. Andrew, a United Methodist congregation in New York City. Over tea and biscuits, Frances-Helen talked to me about her remarkable life.

As a young girl, she lived with her Methodist missionary parents in India, where she observed the cruelty of imperialism: Indian men and women on the streets, with untreated leprosy; British soldiers beating Indians with impunity. Later, her childhood included time in the Depression-era United States and in China under Chiang Kai-shek.

But the toughest years came in Manila, after the Japanese military invaded and occupied the Philippine capital in December 1941. That's when the story recounted at the beginning of this chapter unfolded.

Most of us would probably absolve Frances-Helen and her parents, along with the other men and women who lived in captivity for so long, if they became apologists for at least the selective use of war.

After all, it was brute military force in the Philippines that placed her in danger for so long and claimed an estimated 1,000,000 Filipino lives, in addition to military casualties of 61,000 Americans and 300,000 Japanese.

And it was largely U.S. military power that ended the occupation and led to her liberation.

We'd also excuse Frances-Helen if she ended up hating the Japanese, or at least the Japanese government or army.

But Frances-Helen explained that she and her family made a decision: they would not hate a country or the people of that country; they wouldn't even hate warriors—soldiers, sailors, bomber pilots—who are, after all, also people.

"We decided that we would not hate the Japanese," Frances-Helen remembered. "We would hate only war itself."

Frances-Helen has stayed true to that pledge during a life that has included ordination to the ministry of the United Methodist Church, an option not open to women before 1956.

She took her message many places in the first years after World War II. Many people hungered for her inspiring story of survival, and they got that. But they also heard her testimony against war, all wars.

War pursued by Japan—and war pursued by the United States.

Wars to reverse invasions, and wars to prevent invasions.

Wars in response to terrorism and wars in response to "ethnic" cleansing.

Not specific wars. All wars. Every last one of them.

When a busload of us went to Washington, D.C., in September 2005 to march in a demonstration opposing the war in Iraq, Frances-Helen came along and, three months short of her eighty-first birthday, walked with us. When I visited her in January 2007, at the time I wrote this chapter, she remained resolute that "the single most important issue of our time is the war."

"War harms everybody, even the soldier who is not physically wounded," Frances-Helen said.

She recalled the days in 1945 as the shelling continued in Manila, mortars falling nearby, her father dead, her mother fighting for her life in an emergency field hospital.

As a twenty-year-old American woman, Frances-Helen received a lot of attention from GIs enjoying a few hours of respite from the battlefield. They frequently sat next to her on the steps of the hospital and talked.

"One soldier opened his hand and showed me a small pile of gold," she remembered.

"He had taken it out of the mouths of dead Japanese soldiers on the battlefield. He was really proud of that.

"I wonder if, thirty years later, he reflected on that incident and regretted it. I hope so."

Frances-Helen Foley Guest believes that war remains a plague of humankind because a few people make a lot of money from it. But she is not a hopeless pessimist, noting, "It's amazing how God takes care of us."

"Hate must be taught," Frances-Helen remarks. "A baby smiles at everybody."

And now she thinks that the greater communication made possible by modern technology eventually will overwhelm the tribalism that seems so prominent, especially in time of war.

"The world is smaller; we can't have war anymore," says Frances-Helen. "The oceans can't protect us anymore from a missile; we can't keep war from spreading. We'll just have to find another way."

Frances-Helen Foley Guest is a pacifist with credentials. She's seen war up close, suffered greatly, lost deeply.

Like all pacifists, she's vulnerable to the charge of being naive. And yet, to suggest naïveté in a person who has lived as long and experienced as much as she has seems illogical.

This is a woman whose life experience has brought her the wisdom to know that the absence of war does not equal peace. But it's a good place to start.

I love her stories, her passion, her insight. What I love best is her advice in her sentence: "We'll just have to find another way."

After thousands of years of the genie of war forcing itself out of the bottle, killing people, scorching the land, and teaching hate and suspicion to generations, isn't it about time to try something else?

PRAYER

Eternal God, in whose perfect kingdom no sword is drawn but the sword of righteousness, no strength known but the strength of love: So mightily spread abroad your Spirit, that all peoples may be gathered under the banner of the Prince of Peace, as children of one Father[1]; to whom be dominion and glory, now and for ever. Amen.[2]

PRAYER FOCUS

Picture a world where war is not an option. Think of all the human problems and disputes that would still exist but would need to be resolved another way. Pray to God that you might play a part in that new world.

QUESTIONS FOR REFLECTION

1. In the story above, is the "war" waged by the Japanese, invading and occupying countries throughout the Pacific in 1941, morally equivalent to the "war" waged by the United States in 1945 to end that occupation? Discuss.

2. A true pacifist opposes war in every case. Discuss the implications of renouncing force in all circumstances, given the fact that there are terrible acts of violence committed at various times against innocent people who deserve to have that violence against them stopped.

3. Throughout history, nations at war have talked about seeking the "moral high ground" or "winning the hearts and minds" of the ordinary people. Do you think civilians suffering through the violence of war or, at best, an occupation by foreign power, can make that distinction between the "good" side and the "bad" side? Explain.

---

1. The word *Parent* may be substituted for *Father*.

2. From the Book of Common Prayer (New York: Church Hymnal Corporation and The Seabury Press, 1979). Prayers from the Book of Common Prayer are in the public domain and may be printed and used by Christians of any denomination. Because the prayers are in traditional language, you may want to adapt the language for current usage and inclusiveness.

Epilogue

The writing of this book evolved, starting with some journal notes in reaction to the start of the war in Iraq in March 2003. As I compose this epilogue, exactly four years have passed.

A few weeks ago, the United States began increasing the number of its troops in Iraq, in what was called a surge by supporters of the strategy, and an escalation by its detractors.

It occurred to me that humankind has a remarkable, sustained confidence in the use of force as a "problem solver."

If 140,000 soldiers aren't enough, maybe 160,000 will be.

If the smaller hammer left you disappointed, surely a bigger hammer will work.

Yes, we do have a remarkable, sustained confidence in the use of force as a problem solver. And, perhaps, too much confidence in ourselves.

I've been thinking more about that after a brief, rather strange experience I had flying at 37,000 feet in a jetliner, on a work assignment, when I suddenly looked outside the window at an unbroken floor of fluffy, irregularly shaped clouds lighted by the sun above.

What came to my mind, for reasons that I cannot explain, are words familiar to most Jews, which I am paraphrasing:

> May the One who makes peace in the high places grant peace to all humanity and to Israel. And may all say—
> Amen.

It's not a magic formula—that would let all of us off the hook too easily.

It's a hope. No, more than that, it's a prayer.

Because often we do have too much confidence in ourselves, and, when it comes to war, a very unimpressive track record.

We obviously need some outside help. Let's ask for it.

Like the Catholic women of my childhood, praying their novenas. Praying frequently, faithfully, and feverishly. Believing that their prayers would be answered.

In time of war—especially in time of war—how can we do anything less?

Suggested Reading

As an author, I truly appreciate the willingness of any reader to hang in with me for nine chapters, plus a preface and an epilogue, on the serious issue of war. The folks at Upper Room Books, who know far more about the book business than I, suggest that at least some readers will want to pursue this study further.

So we are including additional resources. The two statements, by the U.S. Catholic Bishops and the United Presbyterian Church, are available online. The four books can be purchased through online booksellers or may be found in libraries.

While I must add the disclaimer that I do not necessarily agree with or endorse the viewpoints expressed, I will say that all six works are relevant to any discussion of war.

The Challenge of Peace: God's Promise and Our Response, U.S. Catholic Bishops, 1983. Available at:

    www.americancatholic.org/Newsletters/CU/ac0883.asp

Peacemaking: The Believers' Calling, The United Presbyterian Church in the United States of America, 1980. Available at:

    www.pcusa.org/peacemaking/believers.pdf

Brimlow, Robert W. *What About Hitler?: Wrestling with Jesus' Call to Nonviolence in an Evil World.* Ada, MI: Brazos Press, 2006.

Hedges, Chris. *War Is a Force That Gives Us Meaning.* New York: Random House, 2003.

Marrin, Albert, ed. *War and the Christian Conscience: From Augustine to Martin Luther King, Jr.* Washington, DC: Regnery Publishing, Inc. 1971 and 1988 (the latter published under the Gateway Editions imprint).

Swartley, Willard M. *Covenant of Peace: The Missing Peace in New Testament Theology and Ethics.* Grand Rapids, MI: Wm. B. Eerdmans, 2006.

Just War Theory
Anderson, David Earl. "Not a Just or Moral War," *Sojourners* (January–February 2003).

About the Author

JIM MELCHIORRE, an Emmy Award–winning television journalist and producer, lives in New York City with his wife, Cheryl Allen Melchiorre, who teaches piano to elementary school students. They have three sons, born in three different decades (to the same two parents): Dan, who works for the Department of Finance of the City of New York; Matt, an audio technician and guitar teacher; and Mark, a student in the New York City public schools.

Jim is the author of *Reflections of Messiah: Contemporary Advent Meditations Inspired by Handel* (Upper Room Books, 2003). He holds a BA degree from Pennsylvania State University and an MS from Pace University. In addition to his many years as a journalist, Jim served in the U.S. Navy and has been active in lay volunteer mission movements since the mid-1980s. He has traveled extensively in the United States and in more than two dozen foreign countries.

Jim Melchiorre (at left) in Kuwait, 1991

Other Titles of Interest

To order any of the following titles, call 1-800-972-0433
Monday through Friday, 8:00 a.m.–4:30 p.m. Central time, or
visit us at www.upperroom.org/bookstore

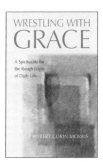

Wrestling with Grace
*A Spirituality for the Rough Edges
of Daily Life*
by Robert Corin Morris

Experience new insights into the daily
practice of Christian spirituality by over-
coming obstacles with grace and open-
ing your spirit to deeper joy and love.

ISBN 978-0-8358-0985-6 • Paperback • 256 pages

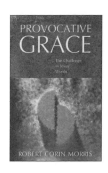

Provocative Grace
The Challenge in Jesus' Words
by Robert Corin Morris

Learn how to focus on the words of Jesus,
not as rules to live by, but as challenges
to provoke you to grow toward greater
maturity.
ISBN 978-0-8358-9848-5 • Paperback • 176 pages

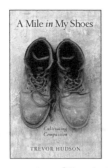

A Mile in My Shoes
Cultivating Compassion
by Trevor Hudson

Discover the possibilities of being on a pilgrimage in your own community through the experience of Trevor Hudson, a pastor and one of the leading voices of reconciliation in the Christian community of South Africa.

ISBN 978-0-8358-9815-7 • Paperback • 128 pages

Listening to the Groans
A Spirituality for Ministry and Mission
by Trevor Hudson with Stephen Bryant

In this short but powerful book, Trevor Hudson calls us to reject spirituality that is only inward, personal, and individual and to pray our way toward a broader understanding of the Spirit that lives and moves among us. Hudson challenges us to listen for those moments when "the world groans in pain and hope" and to respond with both prayer and action in faithful and compassionate living.

ISBN 978-0-8358-9933-8 • Paperback • 64 pages

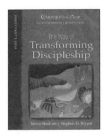

The Way of Transforming Discipleship
by Trevor Hudson and Stephen D. Bryant

This six-week *Companions in Christ* study challenges Christians to live the whole gospel by connecting spirituality and discipleship. Trevor Hudson shares lessons that will help Christians everywhere become agents of truth-telling and reconciliation.

Participant's Book
ISBN 978-0-8358-9842-3 • Paperback • 96 pages
Leader's Guide
ISBN 978-0-8358-9841-6 • Paperback • 96 pages

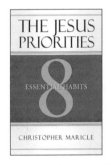

The Jesus Priorities
8 Essential Habits
by Christopher Maricle

"What would Jesus do?" is a great guiding question for living the Christian life, but it presupposes that we know the Bible well enough to come up with the answer. Maricle helps by mapping out the main priorities Jesus modeled in his life and ministry. He shapes these principles into a handbook for discerning right living in relation to God and others according to the ministry of Christ.
ISBN 978-0-8358-9914-7• Paperback • 144 pages

To Walk in Integrity
Spiritual Leadership in Times of Crisis
by Steve Doughty

Through poignant stories, *To Walk in Integrity* offers a model of spiritual leadership in an age of great need. Using illustrations from personal and biblical encounters, Doughty describes the spiritual qualities of those who walk in integrity.

ISBN 978-0-8358-9885-7 • Paperback • 144 pages

Talking in the Dark
Praying When Life Doesn't Make Sense
by Steve Harper

Nothing daunts Steve Harper in this wrangle with God. No doubt, experience, or unholy feeling is out of bounds as he explores the dark passages of life and in prayer. Yet he assures readers that no matter how lost they may feel, they are not wanderers in life's trackless desert but pilgrims through prayer's wilderness of mystery and grace.

ISBN 978-0-8358-9922-2 • Paperback • 136 pages

Every day . . .
   find a way to
      practice the presence of God.

The Upper Room Daily Devotional Guide encourages nearly three million persons worldwide to spend time with God each day through prayer, scripture reading, and meditation. It was "prayed into existence" by a women's prayer group from San Antonio in 1935, and is now available in more than 80 countries.

The reader-written meditations are submitted by people from around the world. *The Upper Room* is available as a magazine or as an online publication. It's also available in Large Print and Spanish (*El Aposento Alto*). A perfect gift for family, friends, and even yourself. Subscribe today.

For subscription information, see
www.UpperRoom.org/subscribe

or

call 1-800-925-6847 for individual subscriptions
1-800-972-0433 for group orders